Janet Rehfeldt

# Terrific
# Toe-Up Socks
## KNIT TO FIT

Martingale®
& COMPANY

Terrific Toe-Up Socks: Knit to Fit
© 2011 by Janet Rehfeldt

Martingale & Company®
19021 120th Ave. NE, Suite 102
Bothell, WA 98011-9511 USA
www.martingale-pub.com

## CREDITS

President & CEO • Tom Wierzbicki
Editor in Chief • Mary V. Green
Managing Editor • Tina Cook
Developmental Editor • Karen Costello Soltys
Technical Editor • Ursula Reikes
Copy Editor • Marcy Heffernan
Design Director • Stan Green
Production Manager • Regina Girard
Illustrators • Timothy Maher & Laurel Strand
Cover & Text Designer • Regina Girard
Photographer • Brent Kane

Printed in China
16 15 14 13 12 11      8 7 6 5 4 3 2 1

**Library of Congress Cataloging-in-Publication Data
is available upon request.**

ISBN: 978-1-60468-019-5

## MISSION STATEMENT

*Dedicated to providing quality products and service to inspire creativity.*

# Contents

4    Introduction

4    The Anatomy of Socks

5    Before You Begin

9    Casting On

13    Working the Toe and Foot

16    Working the Heels

24    Working the Leg and Cuff

26    Binding Off

29    Projects

30    The Boyfriend

33    Marled Zigzag

37    Tide Pools

40    Easily Spectacular

44    Cabled-Rib Yoga and Spa Socks

47    Mardi Gras

50    Faux Cables

53    Beaded and Purled

57    Winterscape

61    Abbreviations and Glossary

62    Standard Yarn Weights

62    Resources

63    Acknowledgments

64    About the Author and Illustrator

# Introduction

Making socks from the toe up remains my favorite way of knitting or crocheting socks. Never fond of finishing work, I love having practically no finishing to do and no grafting of toes. And custom fitting a sock worked from toe to cuff is easier than fitting a sock worked from the cuff downward. For those new to short-row heels, the step-by-step tutorial will have you comfortable with short rows in no time, and toe up may become your favorite method of knitting socks, too.

I've always strived to give knitters choices, and as in *Toe-Up Techniques for Hand-Knit Socks* (Martingale & Company, 2008), multiple methods are given for casting on, increasing, working short rows, and binding off. For those who prefer a heel flap and gusset over a short-row heel, step-by-step instructions walk you through a very good version of a reverse heel flap with gusset.

In *Terrific Toe-Up Socks*, I've included the Mediterranean (or Turkish) cast on, an afterthought heel, some new and revised illustrations and instructions, and all-new sock designs. I hope you enjoy the technique of knitting your socks from the toe up as much as I've enjoyed putting this resource together for all you wonderful sock knitters out there. Happy knitting!

—*Janet Rehfeldt*

# The Anatomy of Socks

Socks knit from the toe up can be worked with a short-row heel, an afterthought heel, or a heel flap and gusset. And although the afterthought heel and short-row heel are similar, each heel style has a distinctive look.

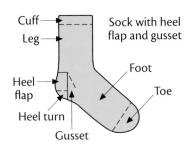

# Before You Begin

Before you dive into the techniques of knitting your socks from the toe up, this section will help you choose yarn and decide what size sock to knit, as well as explain the tools you need (or may want) to make your socks, and the ins and outs of working with double-pointed needles.

## SOCK YARNS

Sock yarns are available in a wide variety of fiber and color combinations: solids, stripes, Fair Isle, jacquard, or random effects, with fiber contents such as bamboo, soy, silk, alpaca, wool, cotton, acrylic, and even chitin (fiber derived from the outer skeleton of insects and shrimp and crab shells). And some yarns even pamper us with jojoba and/or aloe vera.

Yarns designed specifically for sock knitting usually contain nylon or polyamide. When using a yarn with no nylon or polyamide content, you may want to knit elastic or Woolly Nylon serger thread into the cuff. If you choose to reinforce the heel and toe area, reinforcement yarn is available in a good color range for knitting together with your sock yarn as you work the heels and toes.

If you have allergies to particular fibers, be sure to check the fiber content on the label, as even some cotton sock yarns may contain wool or other fibers.

When working with self-patterning and striping yarns, be sure to begin each sock with the same color sequence for matching socks.

## CHOOSING YOUR SIZE

Toe-up socks are often referred to as "knit to fit" or "until the yarn runs out" socks. One of the greatest benefits of knitting toe-up socks is being able to try them on and make adjustments as you knit. You work toe increases to fit at, or just short of, the base of the little toe. The sock foot is knit to just below the anklebone, or 2" to 2½" less than your total foot measurement. After working the heel, you knit the leg and cuff until they reach the length you want—or until you run low on yarn.

To measure a foot for socks (see illustration on page 6), first measure the circumference of the foot at, or slightly above, the base of the little toe (A). Measure the circumference of the foot at the widest point (B). Use these measurements to determine when to stop toe increases and if you need to increase at the instep area.

Next, measure the length from the back of the heel to the tip of the longest toe while the person is standing (C). Use this measurement to determine when to begin the heel; work the sock foot portion until it's approximately 2" to 2½" shorter than the length of your foot.

Hand-knit socks have a degree of stretch, so you do not knit them to the exact circumference and length of the foot. The finished sock foot length should be approximately ¾" to 1" shorter than your foot, and the circumference approximately ½" to 1" narrower than your foot.

When knitting toe-up socks from a specific pattern with multiple sizes, choose the size closest to your foot circumference. If your foot measurement is between sizes, choose the size providing the fit you want; smaller for a snug fit, wider for a loose fit.

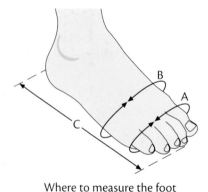

Where to measure the foot

## TOOLS

A set of double-pointed needles and some sock yarn will have you well on your way to knitting your socks. However, besides the basic must-haves for your knitting bag, there are some great tools and gadgets on the market that can be helpful.

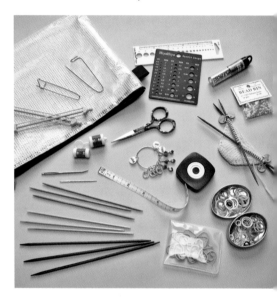

**Double-pointed needles (dpns)** come in different lengths, ranging from 3" to 12", in packages of four, five, or six needles. I prefer 6"-long needles for knitting socks, as some of the longer needles can interfere with each other while I'm trying to work. I normally work with birch or bamboo needles for wool and wool blends, but prefer coated aluminum needles for cotton. There are also plastic flexible needles that work quite well with most yarns. Use the needles you're most comfortable with, at the length you find the easiest to handle.

Although I prefer to knit my socks on double-pointed needles, for those who enjoy working with a single or two circular needles, the techniques in this book will work for you as well.

**Row counters** will help track increases, decreases, and pattern repeats.

**Closed-ring stitch markers** are handy for lace or pattern repeats and for marking increases for reverse heel flap and gusset sections. If you're new to knitting socks, novelty stitch markers with the numbers 1, 2, and 3 are great for marking each needle for the placement of your needles. There are also specialty markers for indicating which types of increases and decreases to make.

**A tape measure** is a must for any knitter's bag and is needed for measuring your gauge and taking measurements while fitting your socks.

**Small- or medium-sized stitch holders** are helpful when working heel stitches. Putting the front foot stitches onto a holder while working the heel gives you flexibility and makes the heel easier to knit.

**Scissors** are needed to cut yarn ends. Yarn-cutter pendants are very handy while traveling.

**Tapestry needles** with large eyes and blunt ends are good for weaving in ends and working a tubular or sewn bind off.

## WORKING WITH DOUBLE-POINTED NEEDLES

Working with double-pointed needles is a bit different than working in the round on a circular needle. At first you may find them a bit cumbersome, like picking up chopsticks for the first time; however, with a bit of patience and practice I think you'll find working with double-pointed needles will become quite easy.

*Tension Tips*

*If you find your tension is just a bit too loose or too tight, try replacing one of the needles with a needle one size smaller or larger to adjust and even out your work. This smaller or larger needle migrates around the work as you knit and can help keep your stitches even. This works best when using needles smaller than US 7 (4.50 mm) and when there is only a .25 mm difference between sizes.*

The information in this book is written for using four double-pointed needles. Three needles hold the stitches while the fourth needle is used to work the stitches. This means you work in a triangular shape and the stitches are divided with half of the stitches on one needle and the other half of the stitches split between the other two needles. The two needles (needles 1 and 3) with fewer stitches hold the sole, heel, and back leg of the sock, while the needle with the larger number of stitches (needle 2) holds the top (or front) foot, top instep, and front leg of the sock.

Once you're set up with your stitches on three needles and have the right side of the work facing you, you'll work the stitches on needle 1 (back left-half section of the sock) with your fourth needle. When all the stitches on needle 1 have been worked, use the now-empty needle to work the stitches on needle 2 (the front foot stitches). When all the stitches on needle 2 have been worked, use that empty needle to work the stitches on needle 3 (the back right-half section of the sock). You're now knitting your sock in the round on double-pointed needles.

Continue working around in this manner, making sure the right side of the work is facing you.

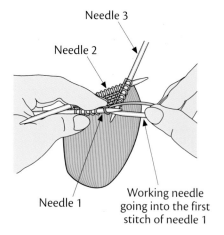

Needle 3

Needle 2

Needle 1

Working needle going into the first stitch of needle 1

### Closing the Gaps

*When working in the round with double-pointed needles, you might find ladders or stranded gaps forming between the stitches when you change from one needle to the next. To help eliminate this, after working the first stitch on each needle, pull it snug.*

Typically, the cast on ranges from 6 to 16 stitches, depending on the weight of yarn and how wide you want your toe. At first, I always worked my toe-up socks with a wrapped cast on. However, I usually needed to tighten up the toe, stitch by stitch, so my preference now is for a closed-toe cast on. I've included the instructions for a Mediterranean (wrapped) cast on along with two versions of a closed-toe cast on. Try each one; then choose the cast on you're most comfortable with.

## MEDITERRANEAN CAST ON

This cast on is also called an Eastern or Turkish cast on. For this cast on, you'll be wrapping the yarn around two needles.

1. Hold two needles parallel along with the tail of the yarn in your left hand. Place the yarn between, then to the back of the two needles. Leaving a tail of about 6", wrap the working end of the yarn over the top needle; take the yarn under the bottom needle, *around and over the top needle, and then under the bottom needle.*

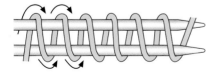

2. Repeat this process from * to * until you have six loops on both needles, counting the first tail wrap as a stitch and ending with the last wrap under the bottom needle. Allow the end of the yarn tail to hang without twisting it into the stitches or tying it off.

3. To knit the loops, begin with the topmost needle and knit through the front of the loop as you would to make a normal knit stitch. The last loop on the top needle is part of the tail, which is just looped over the needle; knit into it as if it were a full stitch.

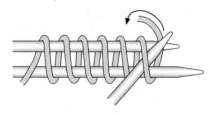

4. Rotate the needles clockwise to work into the loops on the other needle. The first wrap is just draped over the needle. Making sure not to drop the last stitch made on the first needle, knit this first loop; then knit all the loops through the front of the loop as

you did on the first needle, so as not to form twisted stitches.

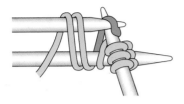

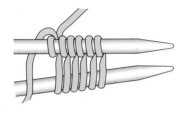

Note that if the stitches are loose, you can tighten them after several rounds of the toe have been knit, or when the sock is finished, by pulling up on the strands one by one until the stitches come together to the same size as your other knit stitches.

5. To add the third needle, knit half the stitches from the first needle (this becomes needle 3). You are now at the center of the back foot stitches, which will be the beginning of your rounds. See page 8 for an illustration of needle order.

## CLOSED-TOE CAST ON

Closed-toe cast ons are, by far, my favorite method for working socks from the toe up. Before beginning the closed-toe cast on, you need to get your first set of stitches onto the needle. The following closed-toe cast-on methods use a long-tail cast on (also referred to as the double-tail, fly-cast, or slingshot method), so let's review that first.

### Long-Tail Cast On

Make a loop with a slipknot and place the loop on the needle. Holding the needle in your right hand, bring the thumb and forefinger of your left hand between the two tails of the yarn and hold onto both tails of the yarn with that hand. Continuing to hold onto the yarn tails, bring the needle down between your thumb and forefinger. The needle will be over the yarn tails, forming loops on your thumb and forefinger, and you'll have what looks like a slingshot.

Following the arrows in the illustration, bring the needle under the yarn on your thumb and into the loop, up along the thumb, over the top and down through the loop on your forefinger, and then down through the loop on your thumb. Pull up a bit on the yarn tails to form the first stitch, but not too tightly as you'll need to knit into the bottom and top of each stitch. Continue to work in this manner until you have the number of stitches you need. You may have to reposition your thumb and forefinger a few times before you get the hang or flow of the cast on.

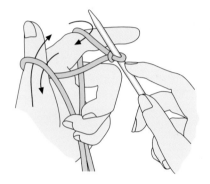

### Closed-Toe Cast On 1

This cast-on method is done by working into the purl bump of each stitch. It creates a very smooth toe on the inside of the sock, which feels good on the foot. The beginning of the toe has small vertical stitches between the first two rounds, but depending on the needle size and yarn used, you might have a hard time seeing them, so it's still a nice-looking toe.

1. Using the long-tail method, cast on eight stitches. Knit one row. Turn the work so the cast on is sitting along the top of the needle, knit side facing you. Working across half of the stitches, knit into the purl bump at the base of each stitch, placing each new stitch

onto a second needle, keeping the original stitches on the first needle.

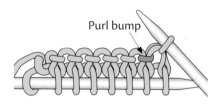

Purl bump

2. When you have knit half of the stitches, begin using a third needle to work into the purl bumps of the remaining four stitches. Turn the work and knit all eight stitches off the original needle, using only one needle to knit them (this will be the front of the foot, needle 2).

3. To get to the center back of the foot for the beginning of your rounds, knit the stitches on the next needle. You should now be at the center back of the foot with needle 1 (the back-left side of the sock) as your beginning point and ready to begin increases at the side edges for toe shaping.

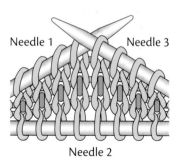

Needle 1          Needle 3

Needle 2

### Closed-Toe Cast On 2

1. Using the long-tail method, cast on ten stitches and turn the work so the cast on is sitting on top of the needle, knit side facing you. Knit into the bottom two loops of the first stitch on the needle, working into the base of the cast on as shown. You're working between the knitted stitches into what appears to be a chain stitch (not the purl bump) and placing each new stitch onto a second needle.

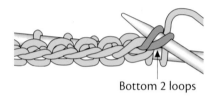

Bottom 2 loops

2. Knit half the stitches onto one needle (this will be needle 3, the back right-side section of the sock).

3. Using a third needle, knit the other half of the stitches onto the new needle (this will be needle 1; the back left-side section of the sock). Work the last stitch into the loop of the stitch on the first needle.

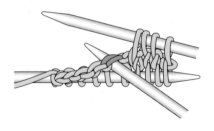

4. Turn the work and knit all ten stitches from the original needle using only one needle (this will be needle 2; the front foot section). To get to the center back of the foot for the beginning of your rounds, you need to knit the stitches on the next needle. You should now be at the center back of the foot with needle 1 (the back left-side section of the sock) as your beginning point and ready to begin increases at the side edges for toe shaping.

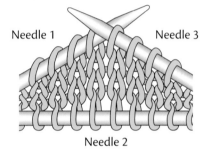

Needle 1          Needle 3

Needle 2

Once you've completed the cast on, you're ready to begin increasing for your toe shaping. You want your toe increases to be symmetrical, so you need to work left-slanting (M1L) and right-slanting (M1R) increases in the proper places. Just remember this mantra: When you reach the end of a needle, work a left-slanting increase. When you're at the beginning of a needle, work a right-slanting increase.

I've included three different ways of working increases. Try each increase method; then pick the one that works best for you or has the finished look you want for your toe shaping.

## RAISED INCREASES

Also known as strand increases, these increases are worked into the strand or horizontal bar located between two stitches.

### Left-Slanting Raised Increase

Insert the left-hand needle from front to back under the horizontal bar between the last stitch worked and the next stitch, lifting the bar onto the left needle. Knit into the back of the stitch.

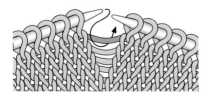

### Right-Slanting Raised Increase

Insert the left-hand needle from back to front under the horizontal bar between the last stitch worked and the next stitch, lifting the bar onto the left needle. Knit into the front of the stitch.

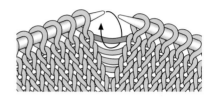

## YARN-OVER OR CLOSED-EYELET INCREASES

These increases are similar in appearance and method to the raised increases. They're very nice looking and seem to give me the most consistency in the look and size of my increased stitches.

### Left-Slanting Yarn Over

Wrap the yarn over the needle from back to front. On the next round, knit into the front of the stitch, twisting the stitch so you don't leave a hole or eyelet.

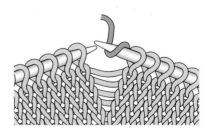

### Right-Slanting Yarn Over

Bring the yarn forward, yarn over the needle from front to back. On the next round, knit into the back of the stitch, twisting the stitch so you don't leave a hole or eyelet.

### Right-Slanting Lifted Increase

Insert the right-hand needle into the back hump or purl bump of the stitch below the next stitch to be worked and knit into it. (You're working in the row below.)

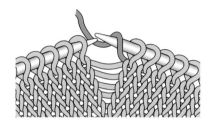

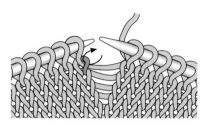

## LIFTED INCREASES

Rather than using the strand or bar between the stitches, these increases are worked into the back (or side) of a previous stitch. The increased stitches are quite smooth, but if you pull them too tight, they can pucker your toe shaping.

### Left-Slanting Lifted Increase

With the left-hand needle, working from the back toward the front, pick up the side loop of the stitch just below the stitch just knit and knit into it. (You're working in the row below.)

## HOW MUCH TO INCREASE

Once you've chosen your favorite increase, you'll work your increases on every other round. Working an even round between increase rounds gives you a nicely shaped and rounded toe. This is also where "fit as you knit" begins to come into play. Keep trying on your sock toe until it is slightly shorter than where the little toe joins the foot. It should fit your foot (or the foot of the person you're making the socks for) snugly but not tight. If you're working from a specific pattern, work your toe increases until you have the number of stitches in the pattern that best fits your foot.

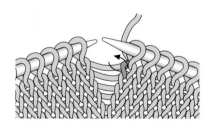

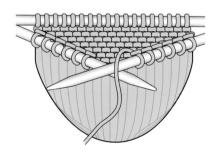

## WORKING THE FOOT

Once you've finished the toe increases and the sock toe fits the foot and/or has the number of stitches required in your pattern, it's time to move on to the foot of your sock.

The foot of the sock is knit in the round with the right side facing you until it reaches just below the bottom of the ankle bone or is approximately 2" to 2½" shorter than the foot measurement taken from the back of

the heel to the tip of the longest toe while standing.

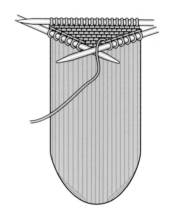

# Working the Heels

The heel of a sock is normally worked on half the total number of stitches on your sock. In other words, if you have 48 stitches, your heel would be worked on 24 stitches. Toe-up socks are generally knit using a short-row or an afterthought heel (see Cabled-Rib Spa Sock, page 44); however, the option of working a reverse heel flap and gusset is covered on page 20.

## SHORT-ROW HEELS

Short-row heels are most like a commercial sock in shape and fit. The heel is worked back and forth, decreasing by using shortened knit and purl rows. You knit or purl to a certain point on the heel stitches, then stop and turn the work, leaving the remaining stitches of that row unworked; thus the term "short row."

You continue working shortened rows until one-third of the original heel stitches are left. You then reknit or repurl the stitches that were left unworked, increasing back to the original number of heel stitches by working one additional stitch on each row.

Instructions are given for three ways of working a short-row heel: working double wraps, working single wraps, and working without wraps.

Short rows leave holes or gaps because of turning your work before the end of a row is completed. There are several methods of eliminating these holes or gaps in the work. In a double wrap, you wrap the stitches as you turn the work on both the decrease and increase sections. In a single wrap, you wrap only on the increase section. The wraps pull in the unworked stitch, closing the gap between the unworked stitch and the stitch next to it. The other method, the "pick method," is covered in "Short Rows without Wraps" on page 19. Typically, I prefer to work double wraps when using very fine yarns, single wraps for worsted-weight yarns, and the Japanese-pick method that uses no wraps when using bulkier yarns, but the choice is really yours.

### Heel Decreases

1. Working only the heel stitches, knit the stitches on needle 1 to the last two stitches, bring your yarn to the front of the work, and slip one stitch purlwise from the left needle to the right needle.

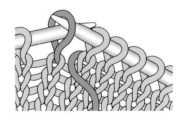

2. Take the working yarn to the back of the work and return the slipped

stitch to the left needle. You didn't knit the stitch; you just wrapped the yarn around it to eliminate holes. You have two stitches that are not knit on needle 1 (the wrapped stitch and the last stitch on the needle).

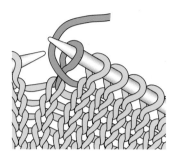

3. Turn your work. The two unworked stitches, are now on the right-hand needle you'll use to purl back across needle 1.

4. Purl across needle 1; then continue to purl across needle 3 (the other side of the heel) until there are two stitches left on needle 3. This time, put the yarn to the back of the work and slip the next stitch purlwise onto the right-hand needle.

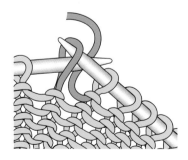

5. Pass the yarn between the needles to the front of the work and return the slipped stitch to the left-hand needle.

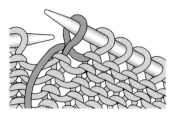

6. You now have four stitches not worked: the two you didn't knit in row 1 and the two you didn't purl in row 2.

Each time you knit or purl a row, work one less stitch, slipping and wrapping that stitch, leaving it unknit or unpurled until the center one-third of the heel stitches are still knit (or active), and all the rest of the stitches on each side of the center stitches have been slipped and wrapped (or put on hold).

---

*Putting Front Stitches on Holder*

*To make life easier while working the heel, I put the stitches from needle 2 (front foot stitches) onto a stitch holder and work the stitches from both needles 1 and 3 (heel section) onto just one needle. It can be less confusing than counting worked and unworked heel stitches on two separate needles plus the needle you're using to knit or purl them with. When I've completed the entire heel, I redistribute the stitches back to the correct needles.*

The next illustration shows the decrease section of the heel, with center heel stitches still in work while stitches on each side of the center have been slipped and wrapped.

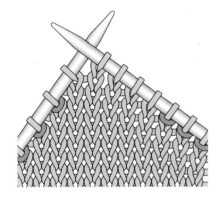

## Heel Increases

After the heel decreases have been completed, you reverse the process, knitting or purling one slipped and wrapped stitch per row until you rework all the stitches in the heel section. To hide the wraps when bringing the slipped stitches back into work, knit or purl the wrap and stitch together as one stitch.

As you rework the original slipped and wrapped stitches, you'll rewrap the next stitch each time you turn the work, so while you're bringing these slipped stitches back into play, you'll have two wraps per stitch.

1. Knit to the closest slipped stitch; then knit that stitch with the wrap together as one stitch.

2. Slip and wrap the next stitch; turn the work.

3. Purl to the closest slipped stitch; purl the stitch and wrap together as one stitch.

4. Slip and wrap the next stitch; turn the work.

Continue working in this manner, repeating steps 1–4 until you've reworked all slipped and wrapped stitches.

**Working the first wraps.** On the very first stitch you knit or purl back into work, there will be only one wrap. Lift the stitch knitwise through the back onto the right-hand needle; then lift the wrap onto the right-hand needle. Slip both the wrap and the stitch onto the left-hand needle without changing their order. Knit or purl them together. Wrap the next stitch and turn the work.

**Working the remaining wraps.** Once you've completed the first knit and purl rows, you'll be working with two wraps per stitch.

1. Lift the knit stitch knitwise through the back, onto the right-hand needle.

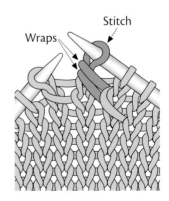

Stitch

Wraps

2. Lift both wraps, one wrap at a time, onto the right-hand needle. Slip both of the wraps and the stitch onto the left-hand needle. Do not change the order of the wraps and stitch when you slip them. Knit or purl the wraps and stitch together as one stitch.

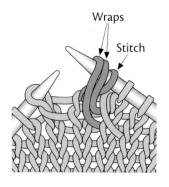

Wraps

Stitch

3. Wrap the next stitch and turn the work. On the next-to-last row on both the knit and purl sides, you'll wrap the very last stitch on each needle before turning.

When all the stitches have been knit or purled back into the work, your heel is finished.

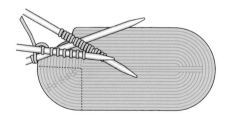

**Single-wrapped short rows.** Single-wrapped short rows use the same principle as double-wrapped short rows; however, you wrap the stitches only once. This method can

leave tiny holes or eyelets along the decrease line, but the result is not as bulky as the double-wrapped short-row method.

To work single-wrapped short rows, do not slip and wrap the stitches when working the heel decreases; simply stop short and turn your work. You slip and wrap the stitches only when working the heel increases, following the same principle as double wraps.

### Short Rows without Wraps

You can work short rows without wrapping the stitches and still eliminate gaps or holes left when turning your work in mid-row. This is sometimes referred to as the pick, catch, or Japanese method. When putting the stitches out of work, do not slip and wrap the stitch, just stop and turn. When bringing your stitches back into work, you pick up the strand between two stitches in the row below and knit or purl the strand together with the stitch. This takes a bit of practice, but once you've done it a couple of times, instinct will take over and you'll know just where to pick up the strands to eliminate the holes.

**Picking on knit rows.** Work to the closest unworked stitch. Using the left-hand needle, pick up the strand between two stitches in the row below on the back (purl side) of the work. Knit the strand and the next knit stitch together as one stitch. You might find it easier to have the purl side facing you when picking up the strand onto the left-hand needle as shown; then turn the work back to the knit side to knit the strand and stitch together as one.

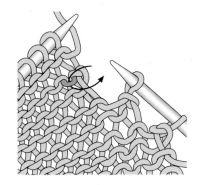

**Picking on purl rows.** Work to the closest slipped stitch. Using the left-hand needle, pick up the strand between two stitches in the row below, reverse the order of the lifted strand and the next stitch to be worked, and purl them together as one stitch.

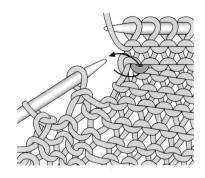

Continue with "Working the Leg and Cuff" on page 24 to finish your sock.

## WORKING A REVERSE HEEL FLAP

Knitting a sock from the toe up does not mean that you always have to do a short-row heel. If you like the feel and shape of the heel flap and gusset associated with a traditional top-down sock, you're in luck. You can work your sock with a reverse heel flap and gusset section.

Socks knit with a reverse heel flap and gusset are worked the same as socks with a short-row heel from the cast on through the foot section, until they reach to just below the ankle bone or are approximately 2" to 3" shorter than the total foot length.

### Gusset Increases and Instep

Because we're working in the reverse of a top-down sock, instead of decreasing at the instep and gusset section, you need to knit the instep even and increase to make a gusset section. Don't panic; you didn't miss anything. The heel flap and turn come later. When working toe-up socks, the gusset increases are worked before creating the heel, increasing on the back foot stitches only, adding two stitches on each increase round with one even round knit between the increase rounds. The front foot (instep) stitches are knit even without increasing.

Use your favorite method for left- and right-slanting increases as you did for the toe. Starting with needle 1, knit up to the last stitch on the needle, work a left-slanting increase; then knit the last stitch on the needle.

Work needle 2 (instep stitches) in your established foot pattern without increasing. On needle 3, knit one stitch, work a right-slanting increase; then knit the remaining stitches on needle 3. Knit one full round without increasing.

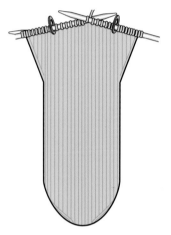

The markers on the illustration are just to show you the original center-back heel stitches located between the markers, and the gusset increases on either side of the markers.

### Gusset Width

Typically, each gusset section should be approximately 1¼" to 2" wide so the sock fits around the heel and instep of your foot. If you have wide ankles, work your gusset section to the full 2" or a bit wider. You don't want the gusset to be too wide, or the sock will be baggy. But if the gusset is too small, the sock will strangle your foot and ankle.

Using your stitch gauge, calculate how many stitches you need by multiplying the number of stitches per inch by the width you want your gusset section. For example, if you want a gusset section measuring 1½" and your stitch gauge is 7 stitches per inch, multiply 7 stitches x 1.5" to determine that you need to increase 10.5 stitches on each side of the heel.

When the number of stitches equals a fraction of .5 or over (one-half a stitch or larger), I round up to the next whole number. In our example, I'd increase 11 stitches at each side of the heel for the 1½" gusset section on each side of the heel.

If the number of stitches needed is less than .5, I simply drop the fraction. For example, if my calculations equal 10.28 stitches, I'd increase 10 stitches at each side of the heel.

To better help you determine how wide to make your gusset, you can use this chart of average gusset widths:

| Narrow-width foot | 1¼" |
|---|---|
| Medium-width foot | 1½" to 1¾" |
| Wide foot | 1¾" to 2" |
| Extra-wide foot | 2" or a bit wider |

### For Wider Gussets

*If you're working a gusset wider than 1¾", work the last three or four sets of increases on every round.*

### Heel Turn

With the gusset and instep complete, it's time to work the heel turn, which is worked only on the original back foot stitches. It does not include the gusset increases. The heel turn is done by working short rows until one-third of the original heel stitches are left in work, while the other two-thirds have been slipped and wrapped, placing them out of work (or on hold).

The decrease section is worked the same as a regular short-row heel, but you'll put two or three stitches on hold for each knit and purl row rather than just one stitch. However, after completing the decreases, you'll bring all the knit and purl stitches back into work in just two rows, rather than one stitch at a time.

1. To make working the heel turn easier, split the front foot (instep) stitches between two needles. Place a stitch marker at the beginning of the front-foot needle located after needle 1 of the back foot, and slip the increased gusset stitches from needle 1 onto that front-foot needle.

2. Place a marker at the end of the front-foot needle that comes just before needle 3 of the back foot, and place the gusset stitches from needle 3 onto that front-foot needle. You should have the original number of heel stitches on both needles 1 and 3 that you had before you began your gusset increases.

### Heel Decreases

The short rows for the heel turn begin on a purl row.

1. Knit across needle 1 with needle 3. Turn the work and purl to two stitches from the end. Following the instructions for wrapping short rows, wrap the next stitch and turn the work (see "Short-Row Heels" on page 16).

2. Knit the heel stitches to two stitches from the end; wrap and turn.

3. Purl the heel stitches to two stitches from the last wrapped stitch. Wrap the next stitch and turn. Knit the heel stitches to two stitches from the last wrapped stitch. Wrap the next stitch and turn.

4. Repeat step 3 until only the center one-third stitches are left in work. For example, if you have 18 total heel stitches, you should have six stitches at the center of the heel still in work, with six stitches wrapped or held on each side of the center stitches.

### Heel Increases

1. To bring the stitches back into the work, purl across the center stitches, then purl all the held and wrapped stitches (making sure to lift and purl the wrap and stitch together as one stitch to avoid holes) up to the last stitch. Purl the last stitch together with one gusset stitch from the front needle.

2. Turn, slip one stitch purlwise, and then knit all the heel stitches (making sure to lift and knit the wrap and stitch together as one stitch on the held and wrapped stitches, to avoid holes) up to the last stitch on the heel. Knit the last stitch together with one gusset stitch from the front-foot needle, knitting the stitches through the back.

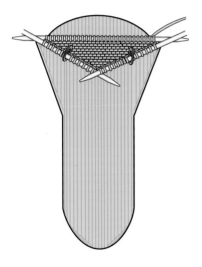

### Heel Flap

The heel flap is knit in the same manner as a traditional basic heel flap; however, you need to incorporate the gusset increases that were temporarily placed on the front-foot needles. Work only the back heel and the gusset stitches. You won't be knitting the original front foot (instep) stitches.

Continue working with the needles as they are: one needle holding the heel stitches and two needles holding the front foot (instep) and gusset stitches.

**Row 1:** Slip one stitch; purl across to the last heel stitch. Purl the last heel stitch together with the next gusset stitch from the front-foot needle. Turn the work.

**Row 2:** *Slip one stitch, knit one; repeat from * to the last heel stitch. Knit the last heel stitch together with the next gusset stitch, knitting the stitches through the back. Turn the work.

Repeat these last two rows, working the last heel stitch together with one gusset stitch until all the gusset stitches have been worked.

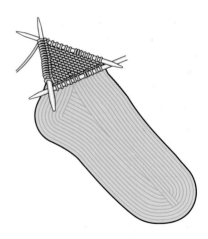

Continue with "Working the Leg and Cuff" to finish your sock.

# Working the Leg and Cuff

Place all the front foot (instep) stitches onto one needle (needle 2), and split the stitches for the back of the sock onto two needles (needles 1 and 3).

## LEG

At this point, you may find you have two small holes where the heel joins the front of the foot on a short-row heel. You can eliminate this in one of two ways, which are described below.

### Closing the Gap: Method 1

One way to avoid a hole on each side of your sock is to pick up the strand between the front- and back-foot needles on the first full round of the leg.

1. Work up to the last stitch on needle 1, slip the stitch temporarily to the right-hand needle, pick up the strand between that stitch and the first stitch on needle 2 (front foot stitches), placing the strand onto needle 1. Slip both the strand and the stitch back to the left-hand needle, and knit them together through the back as one stitch.

2. Work all front foot stitches.

3. Lift the strand between the last stitch on needle 2 and the first stitch on needle 3 up onto needle 3. Knit the strand and the first stitch on needle 3 together through the back as one stitch.

### Closing the Gap: Method 2

Although both methods close the gap, I personally find this second method easier to work, so it tends to be my method of choice.

When I get to the point in my heel where I have only one knit and one purl stitch left that I need to bring back into the work, I work the last two rows of the heel increases differently.

1. Knitting the last knit row of the heel, knit half the stitches of the heel; then use another needle to knit the remaining heel stitches, making sure to pick up and knit the wrap on the last knit stitch. (This is now needle 1, the back left-half section of the sock).

2. Do not turn and purl back. Instead, knit the front foot stitches in pattern onto one needle (remember you either split them onto two needles or put them onto a holder when you began the heel), making that again needle 2.

3. Lift the wrap on the first stitch of needle 3 (the back right-half section of the sock) onto needle 3; then knit the wrap and stitch together as one stitch through the back. Work the remaining stitches on needle 3.

### Finishing the Leg

Knit the leg section in the round, as you did the foot, until the leg reaches the desired height minus the height of your cuff. Remember to read your pattern instructions, as you may now be working all the leg stitches—not just the instep stitches—in your stitch pattern.

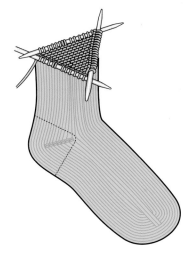

Short-row heel

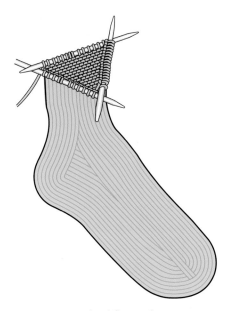

Reverse heel flap and gusset

## CUFF

Cuffs are typically worked in either K1, P1 ribbing or K2, P2 ribbing for 1½" to 2". For a smooth transition, knit one round in stockinette stitch before beginning your cuff if you've worked the leg using a pattern stitch. If your stitch count needs to be altered to accommodate your ribbing, this transition round is the place to do any increases or decreases. Work your cuff to the desired height. Bind off using your method of choice, referring to "Binding Off" on page 26.

# Binding Off

If you've worked a cuff in ribbing, you should bind off in pattern, knitting the knit stitches and purling the purl stitches as you bind off. I generally like to use one needle size larger to work the stitches on the bind-off round, but if you have a tendency to bind off tightly, then use a needle two sizes larger to bind off your socks.

## SIMPLE-RIB BIND OFF

This is a good bind off for either K1, P1 or K2, P2 ribbing. Working slightly loosely, work the first stitch on needle 1; then work the next stitch in knit or purl as if you were continuing in pattern. With the left-hand needle, lift and pass the first stitch over the stitch just worked. Work the next stitch; lift and pass the previous stitch over the stitch just worked. Continue working a stitch and passing the previous stitch over the stitch just worked until you've completed all the stitches. Leaving about a 6" tail for weaving in, cut the yarn and pull the tail through the last loop.

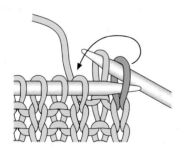

## SUSPENDED-RIB BIND OFF

This is a very stretchy bind off and adds a bit of give if you tend to bind off stitches tightly. The suspended bind off is worked similar to your simple-rib bind off; however, when you lift the first stitch over the last worked stitch, don't drop the stitch off the left-hand needle. Work the next stitch, and then, when allowing the finished stitch to naturally go onto the right-hand needle, drop that first stitch.

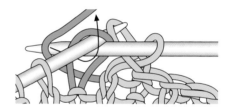

## SEWN BIND OFF

This bind off, also referred to as a grafted bind off, is a good, flexible bind off. You work into each stitch twice, mimicking the knit and purl stitches. The instructions below are for a cuff worked in a K1, P1 ribbing. When you finish the cuff, do not bind or fasten off. Instead, cut the yarn, keeping a tail about four to five times the circumference of the sock.

### Sewn Bind Off: Method 1

1. Thread the yarn tail into a tapestry needle. Assuming the first stitch on needle 1 is a knit stitch, insert the tapestry needle into the stitch as if to purl, *working between the

first two stitches (the knit and purl), take the tapestry needle behind the knit stitch and insert it into the purl stitch as if to knit. Leave the stitches on the knitting needle.

2. Bring your yarn around to the front of the work at the end of the knitting needle, insert the tapestry needle through the same knit stitch as if to knit, and slip the knit stitch off the knitting needle.

3. Bring the tapestry needle and yarn in front of the purl stitch and insert the needle into the next knit stitch as if to purl. Bring the tapestry needle through the purl stitch as if to purl and slip it off the knitting needle.*

Repeat from * to * around the work.

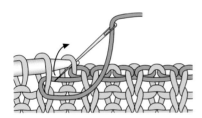

Note that you'll only slip a stitch off the knitting needle after you've worked into it twice with your tapestry needle. When all stitches have been slipped off the knitting needles, fasten off your yarn. To work this bind off on K2, P2 ribbing, begin with a knit stitch; then, rather than working the next purl stitch, work into the next stitch regardless of whether it's a knit or purl. Basically you're just sewing in and out of the stitches, always in the same order, no matter if they're a knit or purl.

## Sewn Bind Off: Method 2

This is similar to method 1 except that you separate your knit and purl stitches onto two needles and work off the two needles. This method is easiest on K1, P1 ribbing, but with a little practice, it's a great bind off for K2, P2 ribbing too.

**For K1, P1, ribbing:** Using two double-pointed needles and working only with those stitches on needle 1, place the knit stitches on one needle and the purl stitches on another needle as follows: Slip the first knit stitch onto one needle, and then place the next purl stitch onto the second needle. Holding the needles parallel, keep the knit stitches on the front needle and the purl stitches in back.

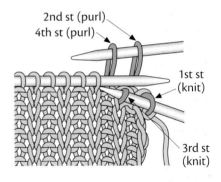

1. Thread the yarn tail into a tapestry needle. Working with a knit stitch first, insert the tapestry needle into the first stitch on the front knitting needle as if to purl, pull the yarn through, and adjust the tension so it's not tight but not sloppy loose. Note that if the first stitch to be bound off is not a knit stitch, slip it to needle 3 to begin with a knit stitch.

2. Working from right to left (front to back), insert the tapestry needle through the back of the last stitch on needle 3. Pull the yarn through, leaving the stitch on its own knitting needle. (You'll work this stitch as the last stitch to be bound off.)

3. Working with the separated knit and purl stitches, insert the tapestry needle from right to left (front to back) through the front of the first purl stitch on the back knitting needle. Pull yarn through, leaving the stitch on the knitting needle.

4. *Insert the tapestry needle from right to left (front to back) through the back of the first knit stitch and, in the same motion from right to left (front to back), through the next knit stitch on the front knitting needle. Slip the first knit stitch off the knitting needle and pull the yarn through.

5. Insert the tapestry needle into the first purl stitch on the back knitting needle from right to left (front to back), and slip the stitch off the knitting needle but keep it on the tapestry needle. Do not pull the yarn through.

6. Insert the tapestry needle from left to right (back to front) through the next purl stitch on the back needle, and pull the yarn through, leaving the stitch on the knitting needle.*

Repeat from * to *, separating additional knit and purl stitches onto two needles as needed. After you've worked about one-third of your stitches, check the stretchiness of the work. If it's too loose or sloppy,

tighten up slightly. If it's too tight, loosen your tension when pulling the yarn through the stitches.

**For a K2, P2 ribbing:** Separate the knit and purl stitches from one sock needle onto two separate double-pointed needles and work the last purl stitch on needle 3 as for step 2 in K1, P1 ribbing, leaving it on knitting needle 3 to be worked last.

1. Insert the tapestry needle into the first knit stitch knitwise; then insert the tapestry needle into the first purl stitch knitwise. *Insert the tapestry needle into the previously worked knit stitch purlwise and, in the same motion, insert the needle into the next knit stitch knitwise, allowing the first knit stitch to drop from the tip of the knitting needle.

2. Insert the tapestry needle into the previously worked purl stitch purlwise and, in the same motion, insert the tapestry needle into the next purl stitch knitwise, allowing the first purl stitch to drop from the tip of knitting needle.*

Rep from * to * until the first set of stitches is complete, and then transfer the next set of stitches and continue from * to * until all stitches are worked.

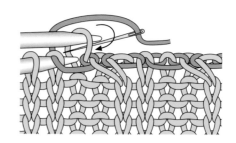

# Projects

The following patterns are written in standard abbreviated format. All short-row heel instructions are written for working with wraps. If you choose to work single-wrap short rows or short rows with no wraps, refer to the short-row heels section beginning on page 16.

If there's an instruction you're unsure of, check the abbreviation list on page 61 and refer to the corresponding section in the book for that instruction. For example, M1L or M1R indicates increasing one stitch as either a left- or right-slanting increase. If you're unsure or want to refresh your memory on left- and right-slanting increases, refer to the toe-shaping section beginning on page 13.

## Designer's Notes for All Patterns

- Each pattern is written for size narrow, with medium, wide, and extra wide listed respectively in ( ) when instructions differ.

- Needles 1 and 3, with fewer stitches, represent the sole, heel, or back of the sock. Needle 2, with the larger number of stitches, represents the front or instep of the sock.

- Heels are normally worked on one-half of the total foot stitches. You may find it easier to work the heel by putting the front foot stitches on a stitch holder.

- If you're knitting both socks from one ball or skein of yarn, you may want to cut the yarn on your first sock, leaving a 4" to 6" tail for weaving in, and then put the stitches onto three stitch holders before knitting the cuff. Knit the second sock until both socks are the same height. Check how much yarn you have left. You may have enough yarn to make your socks taller before working the cuffs.

- For matching socks when using self-patterning and striping yarn, be sure to begin each sock with the same color sequence.

It's the perfect boyfriend sock, with a staggered beginning to the K3, P2 ribbing lending interest and variety to this basic ribbed sock. It's a great sock to learn the ins and outs of toe-up sock construction and short rows, but it has enough variation from a normal two-by-two ribbing to keep your attention. You may end up knitting these socks in your favorite guy colors, as the stretch in this sock allows a fit for a wide range of sizes.

## SKILL LEVEL

Easy ◖■◻◻

## FINISHED MEASUREMENTS

*Due to ribbed stitch structure, sock has about 2" stretch.*

**Circ of leg:** 6⅝ (8, 9¼, 10¼)"

**Circ of foot:** 7 (8¼, 9½, 10½)"

**Height from floor to cuff:** 7½"

## MATERIALS

1 skein of Sock-Ease Yarn from Lion Brand Yarn (75% wool, 25% nylon; 438 yds/400 m; 100 g/3.5 oz) in color 206 Sour Ball (**1**)

Size 2 (2.75 mm) double-pointed needles or size to achieve gauge

Stitch holder (optional)

## GAUGE

8.75 sts and 11.25 rows = 1" in St st

## CAST ON

CO 10 sts (or wraps) using closed-toe CO of choice, ending with 20 sts total after finished CO. Divide sts as follows: 5-10-5.

## TOE SHAPING

**Rnd 1:** *Ndl 1:* knit to last st, M1L, K1; *ndl 2:* K1, M1R, knit to last st, M1L, K1; *ndl 3:* K1, M1R, knit rem sts.

**Rnd 2:** Knit.

Rep rnds 1 and 2, inc 4 sts EOR to 60 (68, 80, 88) sts, then inc 0 (1, 0, 1) st at beg of ndl 2 and 0 (1, 0, 1) st at beg of ndl 3—60 (70, 80, 90) sts. Divide sts as follows:15-29-16 (17-35-18; 20-39-21; 22-45-23).

## FOOT

**Rnds 1–10:** *Ndl 1:* knit; *ndl 2:* K11 (14, 16, 19), P2, K3, P2, K11 (14, 16, 19); *ndl 3:* knit.

**Rnds 11–20:** *Ndl 1:* knit; *ndl 2:* K6 (9, 11, 14), P2, (K3, P2) 3 times, K6 (9, 11, 14); *ndl 3:* knit.

**Rnds 21–30:** *Ndl 1:* knit; *ndl 2:* K1 (4, 6, 9), P2, (K3, P2) 5 times, K1 (4, 6, 9); *ndl 3:* knit.

**Rnd 31 (4th size only):** *Ndl 1:* knit; *ndl 2:* K4, P2, (K3, P2) 7 times, K4; *ndl 3:* knit.

Rep rnd 21 (rnd 31 on 4th size) until sock measures 2" to 2½" less than total foot measurement.

## SHORT-ROW HEEL DECREASES

**Row 1:** Work across ndl 1 to last 2 sts, wyif sl 1 st to LH ndl, wyib return st to RH ndl. Turn work (wrap and turn complete).

**Row 2:** Purl across ndl 1, with same ndl purl across ndl 3 to last 2 sts, wyib sl 1 st to LH ndl, wyif return st to RH ndl. Turn.

**Row 3:** Knit to last 3 sts, sl and wrap next st as in row 1, turn.

**Row 4:** Purl to last 3 sts, sl and wrap next st as in row 2, turn.

Cont to work heel sts, slipping and wrapping an additional st each row until 10 (12, 14, 15) sts have been slipped and/or wrapped on each side of 11 (11, 13, 15) center heel sts.

## SHORT-ROW HEEL INCREASES

**Row 1:** Knit across 11 (11, 13, 15) sts to closest wrapped st, K1 (knitting st and wrap tog as 1 st), sl and wrap next st, turn.

**Row 2:** Purl across 12 (12, 14, 16) sts to closest wrapped st, P1 (purling st and wrap tog as 1 st), sl and wrap next st, turn.

Cont to work heel sts, bringing 1 st back into work each row until all heel sts are worked. On last 2 rows, knit across, wrap last st, turn, purl across, wrap last st, turn.

Knit each of these 2 sts with their wrap tog as 1 st when you come to them *on first rnd of leg.*

## LEG

*Return front sts (ndl 2) to ndl if placed on a holder.*

Knit across ndl 3; ndl 1: knit; sl 3 (1, 3, 1) sts from each end of ndl 2 onto ndls 1 and 3. Mark ndl 2 as beg of rnds. Divide sts as follows: 18-23-19 (18-33-19; 23-33-24; 23-43-24).

Beg with ndl 2, work in K3, P2 ribbing patt on all ndls until leg measures 8" from bottom of heel.

*Loosely* BO in patt. Weave in ends.

Self-striping marled yarn gets an updated look in this zigzag-textured pattern with vivid colors wrapped around a strand of black. The result is a strikingly different and jazzy appearance in a sock that's as comfy as it is appealing to look at. The fold-over cuff accented with tiny buttons adds just the right touch. The pattern also lends itself to solid and hand-painted sock yarns.

## SKILL LEVEL

Intermediate ◐■■▢

## FINISHED MEASUREMENTS

**Circ of leg:** 6¼ (7½, 8⅝, 9⅞, 11)"
**Circ of foot:** 6¼ (7½, 8⅝, 9⅞, 11)"
**Height from floor to cuff:** 7"

## MATERIALS

**MC** 2 (2, 3, 3, 3) skeins of 6-ply Country Color from Regia (75% superwash wool, 25% nylon; 137 yds/125 m; 50 g/1.75 oz) in color 4761 (**2**)

**CC** 1 skein of 4-ply from Regia (75% superwash wool, 25% nylon; 230 yds/210 m; 50 g/1.75 oz) in color 01988 (**1**)

Sizes 2 (2.75 mm) and 3 (3.25 mm) double-pointed needles or size to achieve gauge

16 buttons, ¼" in diameter in coordinated colors

Stitch holder (optional)

## GAUGE

6.5 sts and 8.75 rnds = 1" in patt using larger ndls

## CAST ON

With MC and larger ndls, CO 8 sts (or wraps) using closed-toe CO of choice, ending with 16 sts total after finished CO. Divide sts as follows: 4-8-4.

Knit 1 rnd.

## TOE SHAPING

**Rnd 1:** *Ndl 1:* knit to last st, M1L, K1; *ndl 2:* K1, M1R, knit to last st, M1L, K1; *ndl 3:* K1, M1R, knit rem sts.

**Rnd 2:** Knit.

Rep rnds 1 and 2, inc 4 sts EOR to 40 (48, 56, 64, 72) sts. Divide sts as follows: 10-20-10 (12-24-12; 14-28-14; 16-32-16; 18-36-18).

## FOOT

**Rnd 1 (15):** K1 tbl, P3, *K5 tbl, P3; rep from * around to last 4 sts, K4 tbl.

**Rnd 2 (14):** K2 tbl, P3, *K5 tbl, P3; rep from * around to last 3 sts, K3 tbl.

**Rnd 3 (13):** K3 tbl, P3, *K5 tbl, P3; rep from * around to last 2 sts, K2 tbl.

**Rnd 4 (12):** K4 tbl, P3, *K5 tbl, P3; rep from * around to last st, K1 tbl.

**Rnd 5 (11):** K5 tbl, P3, *K5 tbl, P3; rep from * around.

**Rnd 6 (10):** P1, K5 tbl, *P3, K5 tbl; rep from * around to last 2 sts, P2.

**Rnd 7 (9):** P2, K5 tbl, *P3, K5 tbl; rep from * around to last st, P1.

**Rnd 8:** P3, K5 tbl, *P3, K5 tbl; rep from * around.

**Rnds 9–15:** Work backward from rnd 7 to rnd 1.

Rep rnds 2 through 15 until sock measures 2" to 2½" less than total foot measurement; end with rnd 8 or 15.

## SHORT-ROW HEEL DECREASES

**Row 1:** Work across ndl 1 to last 2 sts, wyif sl 1 st to LH ndl, wyib return st to RH ndl. Turn work (wrap and turn complete).

**Row 2:** Purl across ndl 1 and with same ndl, purl across ndl 3 to last 2 sts, wyib sl 1 st to LH ndl, wyif return st to RH ndl. Turn.

**Row 3:** Knit to last 3 sts, sl and wrap next st as in row l, turn.

**Row 4:** Purl to last 3 sts, sl and wrap next st as in row 2, turn.

Cont to work heel sts, slipping and wrapping an additional st each row until 7 (8, 9, 11, 12) sts have been slipped and/or wrapped on each side of 6 (8, 10, 10, 12) center heel sts.

## SHORT-ROW HEEL INCREASES

**Row 1:** Knit across 6 (8, 10, 10, 12) sts to closest wrapped st, K1 (knitting st and wrap tog as 1 st), sl and wrap next st, turn.

**Row 2:** Purl across 7 (9, 11, 11, 13) sts to closest wrapped st, P1 (purling st and wrap tog as 1 st), sl and wrap next st, turn.

Cont to work heel sts, bringing 1 st back into work each row until all heel sts are worked. On last 2 rows, knit across, wrap last st, turn, purl across, wrap last st, turn.

Knit each of these 2 sts with their wrap tog as 1 st when you come to them *on first rnd of leg.*

## LEG AND CUFF

*Return front sts (ndl 2) to ndl if placed on a holder.*

**Leg:** Knit across ndl 3; *ndl 1:* work est patt, beg with rnd 2 or rnd 7, based on end rnd at beg of heel; *ndl 2:* work in est patt; *ndl 3:* work in est patt.

Cont in est patt on all ndls until leg measures 5" to 5½ " from bottom of heel; end with rnd 8 or 15.

**Cuff:** Work in K2, P2 ribbing for 1½"; do not bind off.

## FOLD-OVER CUFF

With smaller ndls, knit 1 rnd inc 8 sts evenly (2 sts each on ndls 1 and 3; 4 sts on ndl 2); then knit sts on ndl 1. Drop MC—48 (56, 64, 72, 80) sts.

### Right Leg

**Row 1:** Change to CC. With heel facing you, beg with right edge (ndl 3) and knit all sts around, turn.

**Row 2 (WS):** K2, *wyif K2tog tbl; rep from * around to last 2 sts, K2, turn.

**Row 3:** K2, *YO, P2tog; rep from * around to last 2 sts, K2, turn.

Rep rnds 2 and 3 for 2"; end with rnd 2.

**Next row:** Knit, working YOs tbl, turn.

**Next row:** Knit, turn.

*Loosely* BO knitwise. Weave in ends.

Fold cuff over leg, sew buttons on cuff at outer side edges.

### Left Leg

Follow instructions for right leg, reversing beg by having heel facing away from you and attaching CC to beg of ndl 2.

The inspiration for this sock comes from the rocky coastline of northern California, with its waves forming ever-changing patterns etched in sand and fascinating tide pools between the rocks and crevices. A simple wave-patterned lace gently flows along the leg to form tide pools of blues and greens swirling around the foot.

## SKILL LEVEL

Intermediate ■■■◻

## FINISHED MEASUREMENTS

**Circ of leg:** 6½ (7½, 9, 10⅜)"
**Circ of foot:** 6½ (7½, 9, 10⅜)"
**Height from floor to cuff:** 7"

## MATERIALS

2 skeins of Hand-Painted High Twist Sock Yarn from Royale Hare (100% superwash merino; 245 yds/224 m; 56.5 g/2 oz) in color Blue Lake Lily (**1**)

Size 1½ (2.5 mm) double-pointed needles or size to achieve gauge

Stitch holder (optional)

1 stitch marker

## GAUGE

9 sts and 12 rnds = 1" in patt

## CAST ON

CO 10 (10, 12, 12) sts (or wraps) using closed-toe CO of choice, ending with 20 (20, 24, 24) sts total after finished CO. Divide sts as follows: 5-10-5 (5-10-5; 6-12-6; 6-12-6)

## TOE SHAPING

**Rnd 1:** *Ndl 1:* knit to last st, M1L, K1; *ndl 2:* K1, M1R, knit to last st, M1L, K1; *ndl 3:* K1, M1R, knit rem sts.

**Rnd 2:** Knit.

Rep rnds 1 and 2, inc 4 sts EOR to 60 (72, 84, 96). Divide sts as follows: 17-25-18 (17-37-18; 23-37-24; 23-49-24).

## FOOT

**Rnd 1:** *Ndl 1:* knit; *ndl 2:* K1, *K2tog twice, (YO, K1) 3 times, YO, ssk twice, K1; rep from * 2 (3, 3, 4) times; *ndl 3:* knit.

**Rnd 2:** Knit.

Rep rnds 1 and 2 until sock measures 2" to 2½" less than total foot measurement; end with rnd 2.

**1st and 3rd sizes:** Sl 2 sts from ndl 1 to ndl 2; sl 3 sts from ndl 3 to ndl 2.

**2nd and 4th sizes:** Sl 1 st from ndl 2 to ndl 1—30 (36, 42, 48) heel sts.

### Short-Row Heel Decreases

**Row 1:** Knit across ndl 1 to last 2 sts, wyif sl 1 st from LH ndl to RH ndl, wyib sl same st back to LH ndl. Turn work (wrap and turn complete).

**Row 2:** Purl sts on ndl 1, with same ndl, purl to last 2 sts on ndl 3, wyib sl 1 st from LH ndl to RH ndl, wyif sl same st back to LH ndl, turn.

**Row 3:** Knit to last 3 sts, sl and wrap the next st as in row 1, turn.

**Row 4:** Purl across to last 3 sts, sl and wrap the next st as in row 2.

Cont to work heel sts, slipping and wrapping an additional st each row until 10 (12, 14, 16) sts have been slipped and/or wrapped on each side of 10 (12, 14, 16) center heel sts.

### Short-Row Heel Increases

**Row 1:** Knit across center 10 (12, 14, 16) sts to closest wrapped st, K1 (knitting st and wrap tog as 1 st), sl and wrap next st, turn.

**Row 2:** Purl across center 11 (13, 15, 17) sts to closest wrapped st, P1 (purling st and wrap tog as 1 st), sl and wrap next st, turn.

Cont to work heel sts, bringing 1 st back into work each row until all heel sts are worked. On last 2 rows, knit across, wrap last st, turn, purl across, wrap last st, turn.

Knit each of these 2 sts with their wrap tog as 1 st when you come to them *on first rnd of leg.*

## LEG

*Return front sts (ndl 2) to ndl if placed on a holder.*

**All sizes:** Knit across 15 (18, 21, 24) heel sts.

**1st and 3rd sizes only:** Sl 3 sts from each end of ndl 2 to ndls 1 and 3.

**Divide sts as follows:** 18-24-18 (18-36-18; 24-36-24; 24-48-24).

**All sizes:** Knit sts on ndl 1, working wrap with st tog as 1 st when you come to it. Mark ndl 2 as beg of rnds.

**Rnds 1, 3, 5, 7, 9:** * K2tog twice, (YO, K1) 3 times, YO, ssk twice, K1; rep from * around.

**Rnds 2, 4, 6, 8, 10:** Knit.

**Rnds 11 and 12:** Purl.

Rep rnds 1–12 four more times.

*Loosely* BO purlwise. Weave in ends.

... Or spectacularly easy. Not quite a basket weave, not quite a meandering rib, but something in between creates an interesting and easy pattern to walk you through a seamlessly smooth reverse heel flap and gusset. The rich tones of autumn are well suited for this design.

## SKILL LEVEL

Easy ◆■☐☐

## FINISHED MEASUREMENTS

**Circ of leg:** 6⅞ (7⅞, 8⅞, 9⅞, 10⅞)"
**Circ of foot:** 6⅞ (7⅞, 8⅞, 9⅞, 10⅞)"
**Height from floor to cuff:** 7"

## MATERIALS

1 skein of Bearfoot from Mountain Colors (60% superwash wool, 25% mohair, 15% nylon; 350 yds/320 m; 100 g/3.5 oz) in color Yellowstone (❶)

Size 2 (2.75 mm) double-pointed needles or size to achieve gauge

2 stitch holders (optional)

2 stitch markers

## GAUGE

8.25 sts and 9 rows = 1" in patt st

### Foot Pattern

**Rnds 1–6:** *Ndl 1:* knit; *ndl 2:* *K4, P4, rep from * to last 4 (1, 4, 1, 4) sts, K4 (1, 4, 1, 4); *ndl 3:* knit.

**Rnds 7–12:** *Ndl 1:* knit; *ndl 2:* K1, *P4, K4, rep from * to last 3 (0, 3, 0, 3) sts, P3 (0, 3, 0, 3); *ndl 3:* knit.

### Leg Pattern

*Ndl 2 is beg of rnds.*

**Rnds 1–6:** *K4, P4; rep from * around.

**Rnds 7–12:** K1, P4, *K4, P4; rep from * around to last 3 sts, K3.

## CAST ON

CO 10 (10, 10, 12, 12) sts (or wraps) using closed-toe CO of choice, ending with 20 (20, 20, 24, 24) sts total after finished CO. Divide sts as follows: 5-10-5 (5-10-5; 5-10-5; 6-12-6; 6-12-6).

## TOE SHAPING

**Rnd 1:** *Ndl 1:* knit to last st, M1L, K1; *ndl 2:* K1, M1R, knit to last st, M1L, K1; *ndl 3:* K1, M1R, knit rem sts.

**Rnd 2:** Knit.

Rep rnds 1 and 2, inc 4 sts EOR to 56 (64, 72, 80, 88) sts. **(On 2nd and 4th sizes only,** move first st on ndl 3 to ndl 2.) Divide sts as follows: 14-28-14 (16-33-15; 18-36-18; 20-41-19; 22-44-22).

## FOOT

Rep rnds 1–12 of foot patt until sock measures 3 (3, 3, 3½, 3½)" less than total foot measurement.

## GUSSET INCREASES AND INSTEP

**Rnd 1:** *Ndl 1:* knit to last st, M1L, K1; *ndl 2:* work in est patt; *ndl 3:* K1, M1R, knit rem sts.

**Rnd 2:** *Ndl 1:* knit even; *ndl 2:* work in est patt; *ndl 3:* knit even.

Rep rnds 1 and 2, inc gusset 2 sts EOR to 10 (10, 10, 12, 12) sts each side of heel—76 (84, 92, 104, 112) sts total. Note ending rnd of st patt.

**On 2nd and 4th sizes only:** Sl 1 st from ndl 2 to ndl 3.

## HEEL

PM at beg and end of ndl 2, sl 10 (10, 10, 12, 12) sts from ndls 1 and 3 to ndl 2. For easier handling, split sts on ndl 2 onto 2 ndls. With ndl 3, knit across ndl 1, turn. Beg working back and forth on heel sts only.

*Rather than slipping gusset sts to ndl 2, you can use 2 st holders or dpns.*

### Heel Turn

Refer to "Heel Turn" on page 22 as needed.

**Row 1:** Purl across heel sts to last 2 sts, wyib sl 1 st to LH ndl, wyif sl same st back to RH ndl, turn (wrap and turn complete).

**Row 2:** Knit to last 2 sts, wyif sl 1 st to LH ndl, wyib sl same st back to RH ndl, turn.

Cont to short row 2 additional sts, but wrap only 1 st each row until 6 (8, 6, 8, 6) sts have been slipped and/or wrapped on each side of 16 (16, 24, 24, 32) center heel sts.

On next 2 (2, 4, 4, 6) rows, short row 3 additional sts, wrapping only 1 st each row until 9 (11, 12, 14, 15) sts have been slipped and/or wrapped each side of 10 (10, 12, 12, 14) center heel sts.

### Heel Increases

*When working sts with wraps, work st and wrap tog as 1 st. Refer to "Heel Increases" on page 22.*

**Row 1:** Purl across center 10 (10, 12, 12, 14) sts, purl across slipped and wrapped sts to last st, purl last st tog with 1 gusset st. Do not wrap next gusset st. Turn.

**Row 2:** Knit across all sts, working slipped and wrapped sts to last st, knit last st tog with 1 gusset st tbl. Do not wrap next gusset st. Turn.

### Heel Flap

*Sl sts as if to purl. When knitting heel st tog with gusset st, knit the 2 sts tog tbl.*

**Row 1:** Sl 1, purl across to last st, purl last st with 1 gusset st. Do not wrap next gusset st. Turn.

**Row 2:** *Sl 1, K1; rep from * to last st, knit last st with 1 gusset st tbl. Do not wrap next gusset st. Turn.

Rep rows 1 and 2 until all gusset sts have been incorporated into heel sts—56 (64, 72, 80, 88) sts. Do not turn on last rnd.

Return front foot sts to ndl if placed on holders. **On 2nd and 4th sizes only,** sl 1 st from ndl 3 onto ndl 2.

**Next rnd:** *Ndl 2:* work in est patt; K0 (1, 0, 1, 0), *sl 1, K1; rep from * across heel sts. (To eliminate small hole from last heel turn, knit bar between ndls with first st on ndl 3 tog tbl.)

**Next rnd:** *Ndl 2:* work in est patt; knit all heel sts.

Rep last 2 rnds once.

## LEG AND CUFF

*Mark ndl 2 as beg of rnds.*

**(On 2nd and 4th sizes only** sl last st on ndl 2 to ndl 3.) Divide sts as follows: 14-28-14 (16-32-16; 18-36-18; 20-40-20; 22-44-22).

**Leg:** Without disrupting rnd order, work leg patt until leg measures 5 1/2" from bottom of heel flap; end with rnd 6 or 12.

**Cuff:** Work in K2, P2 ribbing for 1½".

*Loosely* BO in patt. Weave in ends.

# Cabled-Rib Yoga
## and Spa Socks

Regardless of whether you're stretching, meditating life's little miracles, or treating yourself to a relaxing day at the spa, the jojoba oil and/or aloe vera treated yarn used in these yoga and spa socks pamper your feet in comfort and style. And don't we all deserve a little pampering?

## SKILL LEVEL

Intermediate ◼◼◼◻

## FINISHED MEASUREMENTS

**Circ of leg:** 7½ (8¼, 9, 9¾, 10½)"
**Circ of foot:** 6¾ (7½, 8¼, 9, 9¾)"
**Height from floor to cuff:** 6"

## MATERIALS

### Yoga Socks

2 skeins Heart & Sole from Coats & Clark (70% superwash wool, 30% nylon; 213 yds/195 m; 50 g/1.76 oz) in color 3935 Tequila Sunrise 🧶**1**

### Spa Socks

1 skein of Step from Austermann (75% superwash virgin wool, 25% nylon; 435 yds/420 m; 100 g/3.5 oz) in color 0120 Margarita 🧶**1**

### Both Socks

Size 2 (2.75 mm) double-pointed needles or size to achieve gauge
Cable needle
1 stitch marker

## GAUGE

8 sts and 11 rows = 1" in K3, P3 flattened ribbing or St st

## CABLE PATTERN

**Cable 3 Front (C3F):** Sl 1 st to cn, P2, K1 from cn.

## YOGA SOCK

### Cast On

Loosely CO 54 (60, 66, 72, 78) sts and divide sts on 3 ndls as follows: 15-27-12 (15-30-15; 18-33-15; 18-36-18; 21-39-18).

Knit 1 rnd.

Knit sts on ndl 1. Mark ndl 2 as beg of rnds.

### Bottom Ribbing

**Rnd 1:** *C3F; rep from * around.

**Rnds 2 and 3:** *P2, K1; rep from * around.

**Rnds 4–9:** Rep rnds 1–3.

### Instep

**Next rnd:** *P3, K3; rep from * around.

Rep last rnd until foot measures 2½" from beg.

Knit all sts for 2 rnds; then rep rnds 1–9 of bottom ribbing.

### Heel Opening and Ankle

**Rnd 1:** *Ndl 2:* *C3F, rep from *; *ndls 3 and 1:* loosely BO all sts.

**Rnd 2:** *Ndl 2:* *P2, K1, rep from *; *ndls 3 and 1:* using twisted-thumb CO, loosely CO 33 (36, 39, 42, 45) sts placing 15 (18, 18, 21, 21) sts on ndl 3 and 18 (18, 21, 21, 24) sts on ndl 1—60 (66, 72, 78, 84) sts.

**Rnd 3:** *P2, K1; rep from * around.

**Rnds 4–12:** Rep rnds 1–9 of bottom ribbing.

### Leg and Cuff

**Next Rnd:** *P3, K3; rep from * around.

Rep last rnd until leg measures 5" from beg of heel opening.

Work rnds 1–9 of bottom ribbing.

*Loosely* BO in patt. Weave in ends.

## SPA SOCK

Work as for Yoga sock through instep, working to 4" from beg of work.

**Next rnd:** Knit.

**Next rnd:** Knit, evenly inc 3 sts each on ndl 3 and ndl 1—60 (66, 72, 78, 84) sts.

Rep rnds 1–9 of bottom ribbing; then work heel opening and ankle, and leg and cuff as for yoga sock.

## OPTIONAL AFTERTHOUGHT HEEL

Beg at center back of foot, PU sts around heel opening as follows: 15 (16, 18, 19, 21) sts onto ndl 1; 30 (33, 36, 39, 42) sts onto ndl 2; 15 (17, 18, 20, 21) sts onto ndl 3—60 (66, 72, 78, 84) sts.

**Rnd 1:** *Ndl 1:* knit to last 3 sts, K2tog, K1; *ndl 2:* K1, ssk, knit to last 3 sts, K2tog, K1; *ndl 3:* K1, ssk, knit rem sts.

**Rnd 2:** Knit.

Rep rnds 1 and 2 until 20 (22, 24, 26, 28) sts rem. On last rnd, knit sts from ndl 1 onto ndl 3.

Turn work so wrong side is facing. Work 3-ndl BO as follows: With knit sts facing tog on 2 ndls, knit first st from each LH ndl tog as 1 st, *knit next st from each LH ndl tog as 1 st, pass first st on RH ndl over next st on RH ndl. Rep from * until all sts are worked. Fasten off. Weave in ends.

### Twisted-Thumb or e-Cast On

*This is an easy way to add stitches to your work.*

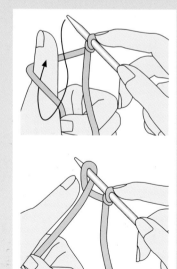

I've always loved stepping out during Mardi Gras, and designing these bright and colorful toe tappers using Mardi Gras colors was especially fun for me. The Fair Isle patterning on the foot and leg are easily accomplished by working with one color at a time, slipping stitches, then knitting or purling them with the next color.

## SKILL LEVEL

Intermediate ◆■■□

## FINISHED MEASUREMENTS

**Circ of foot (unstretched):** 7 (7⅞, 8¾, 9⅝, 10¾)"

**Circ of leg (unstretched):** 7 (7⅞, 8¾, 9⅝, 10¾)"

**Height from floor to cuff:** approx: 8"

## MATERIALS

Alpaca Silk from Blue Sky Alpacas (50% alpaca, 50% silk; 146 yds/133 m; 50 g/1.75 oz) 🄬

**MC** 2 skeins in color 129 Amethyst

**CC** 1 (1, 1, 2, 2) skein in color 141 Peapod

Size 1½ (2.5 mm) double-pointed needles or size to achieve gauge

Stitch holder (optional)

1 stitch marker

## GAUGE

8.5 sts and 12 rows = 1" in patt

*With the exception of the cuff, each rnd is worked in one color.*

## CAST ON

With CC, CO 10 (12, 12, 14, 14) sts (or wraps) using closed-toe CO of choice, ending with 20 (24, 24, 28, 28) sts total after finished CO. Divide sts as follows: 5-10-5 (6-12-6; 6-12-6; 7-14-7; 7-14-7)

## TOE SHAPING

**Rnd 1:** *Ndl 1:* knit to last 2 sts, Kl, M1L, K1; *ndl 2:* K1, M1R, knit to last 2 sts, K1, M1L, K1; *ndl 3:* K1, M1R, knit rem sts on ndl 3—24 (28, 28, 32, 32) sts.

**Rnd 2:** Knit.

Rep rnds 1 and 2, inc 4 sts EOR to 60 (68, 76, 84, 92) sts. Divide sts as follows: 15-30-15 (17-34-17; 19-38-19; 21-42-21; 23-46-23).

## FOOT

*Mark ndl 2 as the beg of rnds.*

Change to MC, knit one rnd.

**Rnds 1 and 2:** With MC, *P2, K2; rep from * around.

**Rnd 3:** With CC, *K2, sl 2; rep from * around.

**Rnd 4:** With CC, *P2, sl 2; rep from * around.

**Rnd 5:** With MC, knit all sts.

Rep rnds 1–5 until sock measures approx 2¼" to 2½" less than total foot measurement. Then rep rnds 1–4 once.

## SHORT-ROW HEEL DECREASES

*Beg working back and forth with CC on heel sts only.*

**Row 1:** With CC purl across ndl 1, with same ndl purl sts on ndl 3 to last 2 sts, with wyib sl 1 st from LH ndl to RH ndl, wyif sl same st back to LH ndl. Turn work (wrap and turn complete).

**Row 2:** Knit across to last 2 sts, wyif sl 1 st from LH ndl to RH ndl, wyib sl same st back to LH ndl, turn.

**Row 3:** Purl to last 3 sts, sl and wrap next st as in row 1, turn.

**Row 4:** Knit across to last 3 sts, sl and wrap next st as in row 2, turn.

Cont to work heel sts, slipping and wrapping an additional st each row until 10 (11, 13, 14, 16) sts have been slipped and/or wrapped on each side of 10 (12, 12, 14, 14) center heel sts.

## SHORT-ROW HEEL INCREASES

**Row 1:** Purl across center 10 (12, 12, 14, 14) sts to closest wrapped st, P1 (purling st and wrap tog as 1 st), sl and wrap next st, turn.

**Row 2:** Knit across center 11 (13, 13, 15, 15) sts to closest wrapped st, K1 (knitting st and wrap tog as 1 st), sl and wrap next st, turn.

Cont to work heel sts, bringing 1 st back into work each row until all heel sts are worked. On last 2 rows, knit across, wrap last st, turn, purl across, wrap last st, turn.

Knit each of these 2 sts with their wraps tog as 1 st when you come to them *on first rnd of leg.*

## LEG AND CUFF

*Return front sts (ndl 2) to ndl if placed on a holder.*

**Leg:** With MC, work rnd 1 of est patt.

Cont est patt until leg reaches 5½" from bottom of heel, ending with rnd 5 of patt.

**Cuff:** Beg cuff patt, working both colors at the same time on each rnd.

**Rnd 1:** With MC, *K2, P2; rep from * around.

**Rnds 2 and 3:** *With CC, K2, with MC, P2; rep from * around.

**Rnds 4–7:** With MC, *K2, P2; rep from * around.

**Rnds 8 and 9:** Rep rnds 2 and 3.

**Rnds 10–13:** With MC, *K2, P2; rep from * around.

**Rnds 14 and 15:** Rep rnds 2 and 3. Drop CC.

**Rnd 16:** With MC, *K2, P2; rep from * around.

*Loosely* BO in patt. Weave in ends.

The simple act of strategically placing decreases and yarn overs creates an intertwining look people will think you spent time and effort cabling. The faux cables are framed with small eyelets for that added touch of lace. Don't want the lace? Simply knit into the back of the yarn overs, twisting the stitch and closing the hole. This pattern also works well with solid colors.

## SKILL LEVEL

Intermediate ◖■■◻

## FINISHED MEASUREMENTS

**Circ of leg:** 6¾ (7¾, 8¾, 9¾)"

**Circ of foot:** 6¾ (7¾, 8¾, 9¾)"

**Height from floor to cuff:** 7½"

## MATERIALS

1 skein of Heritage from Cascade Yarns (75% merino superwash, 25% nylon; 437 yds/400 m; 100 g/3.5 oz) in color 9884 (1)

Size 2 (2.75 mm) double-pointed needles or size to achieve gauge

Stitch holder (optional)

1 stitch marker

## GAUGE

8 sts and 9.5 rnds = 1" in St st

## CAST ON

CO 8 (10, 10, 12) sts (or wraps) using closed-toe CO of choice, ending with 16 (20, 20, 24) sts total after finished CO. Divide sts as follows: 4-8-4 (5-10-5; 5-10-5; 6-12-6).

## TOE SHAPING

**Rnd 1:** *Ndl 1:* knit to last st, M1L, K1; *ndl 2:* K1, M1R, knit to last st, M1L, K1; *ndl 3:* K1, M1R, knit rem sts.

**Rnd 2:** Knit.

Rep rnds 1 and 2, inc 4 sts EOR to 56 (64, 72, 80) sts. Divide sts as follows: 15-26-15 (15-34-15; 19-34-19; 19-42-19).

## FOOT

**Rnds 1 and 2:** *Ndl 1:* knit; *ndl 2:* P2, *K6, P2, rep from *; *ndl 3:* knit.

**Rnd 3:** *Ndl 1:* knit; *ndl 2:* P2, *YO, K2, sl 1-K1-psso, K2, P2, rep from *; *ndl 3:* knit.

**Rnds 4 and 6:** Rep rnd 1.

**Rnd 5:** *Ndl 1:* knit; *ndl 2:* P2, *K1, YO, K2, sl 1-K1-psso, K1, P2, rep from *; *ndl 3:* knit.

**Rnd 7:** *Ndl 1:* knit; *ndl 2:* P2, *K2, YO, K2, sl 1-K1-psso, P2, rep from *; *ndl 3:* knit.

**Rnds 8–10:** Rep rnd 1.

**Rnd 11:** *Ndl 1:* knit; *ndl 2:* P2, \*K2, K2tog, K2, YO, P2, rep from \*; *ndl 3:* knit.

**Rnds 12, 14, and 16:** Rep rnd 1.

**Rnd 13:** *Ndl 1:* knit; *ndl 2:* P2, \*K1, K2tog, K2, YO, K1, P2, rep from \*; *ndl 3:* knit.

**Rnd 15:** *Ndl 1:* knit; *ndl 2:* P2, \*K2tog, K2, YO, K2, P2, rep from \*; *ndl 3:* knit.

Rep rnds 1–16 until sock measures 2½" less than total foot measurement; end with rnd 8 or 16.

**1st and 3rd sizes:** Sl 1 st from ndls 1 and 3 onto ndl 2.

**2nd and 4th sizes:** Sl 1 st from each end of ndl 2 onto ndls 1 and 3—28 (32, 36, 40) heel sts.

## SHORT-ROW HEEL DECREASES

**Row 1:** Work across ndl 1 to last 2 sts, wyif sl 1 st to LH ndl, wyib return st to RH ndl. Turn work (wrap and turn complete).

**Row 2:** Purl across ndl 1, with same ndl purl across ndl 3 to last 2 sts, wyib sl 1 st to LH ndl, wyif return st to RH ndl, turn.

**Row 3:** Knit to last 3 sts, sl and wrap next st as in row l, turn.

**Row 4:** Purl to last 3 sts, sl and wrap next st as in row 2, turn.

Cont to work heel sts, slipping and wrapping an additional st each row until 9 (11, 12, 13) sts have been slipped and/or wrapped on each side of 10 (10, 12, 14) center heel sts.

## SHORT-ROW HEEL INCREASES

**Row 1:** Knit across 10 (10, 12, 14) sts to closest wrapped st, K1 (knitting st and wrap tog as 1 st), sl and wrap next st, turn.

**Row 2:** Purl across 11 (11, 13, 15) sts to closest wrapped st, P1 (purling st and wrap tog as 1 st), sl and wrap next st, turn.

Cont to work heel sts, bringing 1 st back into work each row until all heel sts are worked. On last 2 rows, knit across, wrap last st, turn, purl across, wrap last st, turn.

Knit each of these 2 sts with their wrap tog as 1 st when you come to them *on first rnd of leg.*

## LEG AND CUFF

*Return front sts (ndl 2) to ndl if placed on a holder.*

**1st and 3rd sizes:** Sl 1 st from each end of ndl 2 onto ndls 1 and 3.

**2nd and 4th sizes:** Sl 1 st from ndls 1 and 3 onto ndl 2. Mark ndl 2 as beg of rnds.

Divide sts as follows: 15-26-15 (15-34-15, 19-34-19, 19-42-19).

**Leg:** Work in est patt across ndl 2, cont patt st around entire leg. Work leg in est patt until leg measures 6" from base of heel; end with rnd 8 or 16.

**Cuff:** Work in K2, P2 ribbing for 1½".

*Loosely* BO in patt. Weave in ends.

Eyelet and purled ridges, seed beads, picot edging, and shades of peach in a soft, delicate yarn bring a bit of a bygone Victorian-era style and elegance to this sock. It definitely brings out the feminine side for those days you just feel like a girlie girl.

## SKILL LEVEL

Experienced ●■■▶

## FINISHED MEASUREMENTS

**Circ of leg:** 6½ (8, 9⅝, 11)"

**Circ of foot:** 6½ (8, 9⅝, 11)"

**Height from floor to cuff:** 7"

## MATERIALS

2 skeins of Melody from Jojoland (100% wool; 220 yds/200 m; 50 g/1.76 oz) in color MS41 (❶)

Size 1½ (2.5 mm) double-pointed needles or size to achieve gauge

Approx 144 (180, 216, 252) size 8 seed beads in coordinating color

2 stitch markers

2 stitch holders (optional)

## GAUGE

8.75 sts and 12 rnds = 1" in patt

## CAST ON

CO 10 (10, 12, 12) sts (or wraps) using closed-toe CO of choice, ending with 20 (20, 24, 24) sts total after finished CO. Divide sts as follows: 5-10-5 (5-10-5; 6-12-6; 6-12-6)

## TOE SHAPING

**Rnd 1:** *Ndl 1:* knit to last st, M1L, K1; *ndl 2:* K1, M1R, knit to last st, M1L, K1; *ndl 3:* K1, M1R, knit rem sts.

**Rnd 2:** Knit.

Rep rnds 1 and 2, inc 4 sts EOR to 56 (68, 84, 96) sts. Then inc 0 (1, 0, 1) st at beg of ndl 2; and 0 (1, 0, 1) st at beg of ndl 3—56 (70, 84, 98) sts. Divide sts on 3 ndls as follows: 14-28-14 (17-35-18; 21-42-21; 24-49-25).

## SPECIAL STITCHES

**Yarn over before a knit:** Wyib, yarn over and around the ndl.

**Yarn over before a purl:** Wyif, yarn over and around the ndl.

**Purling a bead (P1b):** Bring bead close to work, insert RH ndl in next st, work purl, pushing bead through st to sit on top of purl bump. On next rnd, hold bead at front of work, knit beaded st through the back.

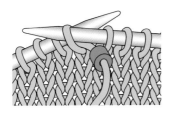

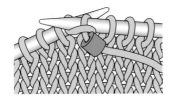

## FOOT

**Rnd 1:** *Ndl 1:* knit; *ndl 2:* *P1, P2tog, YO, K1, YO, P2tog, P1, rep from *; *ndl 3:* knit.

**Rnds 2–4:** Knit.

Rep rnds 1–4 until sock measures 3 (3, 3¼, 3½)" less than total foot measurement; end with rnd 4 (2, 4, 2).

## GUSSET INCREASES AND INSTEP

**Rnd 1:** *Ndl 1:* knit to last st, M1L, K1; *ndl 2:* work in est patt; *ndl 3:* K1, M1R, knit rem sts.

**Rnd 2:** *Ndl 1:* knit; *ndl 2:* work in est patt; *ndl 3:* knit.

Rep rnds 1 and 2, inc gusset 2 sts EOR to 11 (12, 13, 14) sts each side of heel. Note ending rnd of st patt—78 (94, 110, 126) sts.

## HEEL

**2nd and 4th sizes only:** Sl 1 st from ndl 3 to ndl 2.

PM at beg and end of ndl 2, sl 11 (12, 13, 14) gusset sts from ndls 1 and 3 onto ndl 2. For easier handling, split sts on ndl 2 onto 2 ndls. With ndl 3, knit across ndl 1, turn—28 (34, 42, 48) sts.

*Rather than slipping gusset sts to ndl 2, you can use 2 st holders or dpns.*

### Heel Turn

*Refer to "Heel Turn" (page 22) as needed.*

**Row 1:** Purl across heel sts to last 2 sts, wyib sl 1 st to LH ndl, wyif sl same st back to RH ndl, turn.

**Row 2:** Knit to last 2 sts, wyif sl 1 st to LH ndl, wyib sl same st back to RH ndl, turn.

Cont to short row 2 additional sts but wrapping only 1 st each row on heel until 6 (6, 8, 8) sts have been short rowed on each side of center heel sts.

On next 2 (4, 4, 6) rows, short row 3 additional sts, wrapping only 1 st each row until 9 (12, 14, 17) sts have been slipped and/or wrapped each side of 10 (10, 14, 14) center heel sts.

### Heel Increases

*When working sts with wraps, work st and wrap tog as 1 st. Refer to "Heel Increases" on page 22.*

**Row 1:** Purl across center 10 (10, 14, 14) sts, purl across slipped and wrapped sts to last st, purl last st tog with 1 gusset st. Do not wrap next gusset st. Turn.

**Row 2:** Knit across all sts, working slipped and wrapped sts to last st, knit last st tog with 1 gusset st tbl. Do not wrap next gusset st. Turn.

### Heel Flap

*Sl sts as if to purl. When knitting heel st tog with gusset st, knit the 2 sts tog tbl.*

**Row 1:** Sl 1 st, purl across to last st, purl last st with 1 gusset st. Do not wrap next gusset st. Turn.

**Row 2:** *Sl 1 st, K1; rep from * to last st, knit last st with 1 gusset st tog tbl. Do not wrap next gusset st. Turn.

Rep rows 1 and 2 until all gusset sts have been incorporated into heel sts. Do not turn on last rnd.

## LEG

*On first rnd of leg, knit bar between ndls tog with first st on ndl 3 tbl, eliminating small hole from heel turn.*

**Next 2 rnds:** Knit. This should be rnds 3 and 4 of patt.

Mark front foot as beg of patt and work patt around all leg sts.

**Rnd 1:** *P1, P2tog, YO, K1, YO, P2tog, P1; rep from * around.

**Rnds 2–4:** Knit.

Rep rnds 1–4 once; then rep rnds 1 and 2. Cut yarn, leaving 3" to 4" tail, thread half of the beads onto working yarn, reattach yarn at ndl 2, and work rnds 3 and 4 of patt. Beg beading patt as follows.

**Rnd 1:** *P1b, P2tog, YO, K1, YO, P2tog, P1b; rep from * around.

**Rnds 2–4:** Knit.

Rep rnds 1–4 seven more times.

## CUFF

**Rnd 1:** *Sl 1 purlwise, K1; rep from * around.

**Rnd 2:** Knit.

Rep last 2 rnds 3 more times.

**Next rnd:** Purl around, dec 1 (0, 0, 1) st as P2tog.

**Next rnd:** Knit.

**Next rnd:** Purl, turn work.

**Next rnd (WS):** BO 2 sts, *sl 1 st from RH ndl to LH ndl, knit CO 2 sts (see below), BO 5 sts; rep from * around to last 2 (2, 1, 2) sts on leg, knit CO 2 sts, BO all sts. Fasten off. Weave in ends.

---

**Knit Cast On**

*Knit next st, return st to LH ndl.*

Winters spent in the Sierra Mountains and in the Midwest are the inspiration for this sock. Ridges of snowdrifts cascade around the foot while snowflakes and beaded snowdrops fall along the leg, bringing to mind beautiful win-terscapes. The beading is easily accomplished using a crochet hook to place the beads.

## SKILL LEVEL

Intermediate ◼◼◼◻

## FINISHED MEASUREMENTS

**Circ of leg:** 6⅞ (8, 9¼, 10¼)"

**Circ of foot:** 6⅞ (8, 9¼, 10¼)"

**Height from floor to cuff:** 8"

## MATERIALS

Heritage from Cascade Yarns (75% merino superwash, 25% nylon; 437 yds/400 m; 100 g/3.5 oz) (🔢1)

**MC** 1 skein in color 5604

**CC** 1 skein in color 5618

Size 2 (2.75mm) double-pointed needles or size to achieve gauge

Size 11 steel crochet hook for beading

Approx 9 gm size 6/0 beads in silver-lined light crystal blue

1 stitch marker

## GAUGE

8.75 sts and 11 rnds = 1" in St st

## SPECIAL STITCHES

**Cross 2 Left (C2L):** Knit into back of 2nd st, then knit first st, sl both sts off ndl at same time.

**Cross 2 Right (C2R):** Knit into front of 2nd st, then knit first st, sl both sts off ndl at same time.

**Beaded CC Stitch:** Knit st in CC, return st to LH ndl, place bead on crochet hook, insert hook into st, pull st through bead, place st on RH ndl.

## CAST ON

With MC, CO 10 sts (or wraps) using closed-toe CO of choice, ending with 20 sts total after finished CO. Divide sts as follows: 5-10-5.

## TOE SHAPING

**Rnd 1:** *Ndl 1:* knit to last st, M1L, K1; *ndl 2:* K1, M1R, knit to last st, M1L, K1; *ndl 3:* K1, M1R, knit rem sts.

**Rnd 2:** Knit.

Rep rnds 1 and 2, inc 4 sts EOR to 60 (68, 80, 88) sts; then inc 0 (1, 0, 1) st at beg of ndl 2, and 0 (1, 0, 1) st at beg of ndl 3—60 (70, 80, 90) sts. Divide sts as follows: 15-30-15 (17-35-18; 20-40-20; 22-45-23).

## FOOT

**Rnds 1 and 2:** With MC, knit.

**Rnd 3:** With CC, knit.

**Rnd 4:** P6, K3, *P7, K3; rep from * around, P1.

**Rnds 5–7:** With MC, K6, sl 3, *K7, sl 3; rep from * around, K1.

**Rnd 8:** *K5, C2R, K1, C2L; rep from * around.

**Rnds 9–11:** Knit.

**Rnd 12:** With CC, knit.

**Rnd 13:** P1, K3, *P7, K3; rep from * around, P6.

**Rnds 14–16:** With MC, K1, sl 3, *K7, sl 3; rep from * around, K6.

**Rnd 17:** *C2R, K1, C2L, K5; rep from * around.

**Rnd 18:** Knit.

Rep rnds 1–18 until sock measures 2½" less than total foot measurement; end with rnd 2 or 11.

## SHORT-ROW HEEL DECREASES

**Row 1:** Work across ndl 1 to last 2 sts, wyif sl 1 st to LH ndl, wyib return st to RH ndl. Turn work (wrap and turn complete).

**Row 2:** Purl across ndl 1 and with same ndl, purl across ndl 3 to last 2 sts, wyib, sl 1 st to LH ndl, wyif return st to RH ndl. Turn.

**Row 3:** Knit to last 3 sts, sl and wrap next st as in row 1, turn.

**Row 4:** Purl to last 3 sts, sl and wrap next st as in row 2, turn.

Cont to work heel sts, slipping and wrapping an additional st each row until 10 (12, 13, 15) sts have been slipped and/or wrapped on each side of 10 (11, 14, 15) center heel sts.

## SHORT-ROW HEEL INCREASES

**Row 1:** Knit across 10 (11, 14, 15) sts to closest wrapped st, K1 (knit st and wrap tog as 1 st), sl and wrap next st, turn.

**Row 2:** Purl across 11 (12, 15, 16) sts to closest wrapped st, P1 (purl st and wrap tog as 1 st), sl and wrap next st, turn.

Cont to work heel sts, bringing 1 st back into work each row until you've worked all sts. On last 2 rows, knit across, wrap last st, turn, purl across, wrap last st, turn.

Knit each of these 2 sts with their wrap tog as 1 st when you come to them *on first rnd of leg.*

## LEG AND CUFF

*Return front sts (ndl 2) to ndl if placed on a holder.*

Knit across ndl 3 and ndl 1, inc 0 (1, 0, 0) st on each ndl. Mark ndl 2 as beg of rnds—60 (72, 80, 90) sts.

**Leg:** With MC, knit 3 rnds. Beg working with both colors at the same time, following graph (for your size) and using MC for background and CC for motif. Work rnds 16–20 of graph once, then work rows 1–20 of graph 2 times, drop CC.

**Cuff:** With MC work in K2, P2 ribbing for 1" (**4th size only:** dec 2 sts on first rnd for 88 sts).

With CC, work 6 rnds of knit.

*Loosely* BO knitwise. Weave in ends.

**Chart for 1st and 3rd sizes**

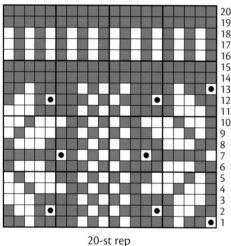

20-st rep

**Chart for 2nd and 4th sizes**

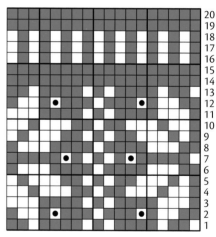

18-st rep

**Key**

■ MC
□ CC
⊡ CC beaded st

# Abbreviations and Glossary

| | | | | |
|---|---|---|---|---|
| **approx** | approximately | | **patt** | pattern(s) |
| **beg** | begin(ning) | | **PM** | place marker |
| **BO** | bind off | | **PU** | pick up and knit |
| **CC** | contrasting color | | **rem** | remain(ing)(s) |
| **CO** | cast on | | **rep(s)** | repeat(s) |
| **circ** | circumference | | **RH** | right hand |
| **cn** | cable needle | | **rnd(s)** | round(s) |
| **cont** | continue(ing)(s) | | **RS** | right side |
| **dec** | decrease(d)(ing)(s) | | **sl** | slip |
| **dpn(s)** | double-pointed needle(s) | | **sl st(s)** | slip stitches purlwise unless instructed otherwise |
| **est** | established | | | |
| **EOR** | every other row or round | | **sl 1-K1-psso** | |
| **g** | gram(s) | | | slip 1 stitch as if to knit, knit 1 stitch, pass the slipped stitch over the knit stitch (1 stitch decreased) |
| **inc** | increase(d)(ing)(s) | | | |
| **K** | knit | | | |
| **K2tog** | knit 2 stitches together as one (1 stitch decreased) | | **ssk** | slip 1 stitch as if to knit, slip 1 more stitch as if to knit, return stitches to left needle and knit them together through the back loop (1 stitch decreased) |
| **LH** | left hand | | | |
| **m** | meter(s) | | | |
| **M1L** | increase 1 stitch using left-slanting increase (page 13) | | | |
| | | | **st(s)** | stitch(es) |
| **M1R** | increase 1 stitch using right-slanting increase (page 13) | | **St st(s)** | stockinette stitch(es) |
| | | | **tbl** | through back loop(s) |
| **MC** | main color | | **tog** | together |
| **mm** | millimeter(s) | | **WS** | wrong side |
| **ndl(s)** | needle(s) | | **wyib** | with yarn in back |
| **oz** | ounce(s) | | **wyif** | with yarn in front |
| **P** | purl | | **yd(s)** | yard(s) |
| **P2tog** | purl 2 stitches together as one (1 stitch decreased) | | **YO(s)** | yarn over(s) |

# Standard Yarn Weights

| Yarn-Weight Symbol and Category Name | 0 | 1 | 2 | 3 |
|---|---|---|---|---|
| Types of Yarn in Category | Fingering, 10-count crochet thread | Sock, Fingering, Baby | Sport, Baby | DK, Light Worsted |
| Knit Gauge Range* in Stockinette Stitch to 4" | 33 to 40 sts | 27 to 32 sts | 23 to 26 sts | 21 to 24 sts |
| Recommended Needle in U.S. Size Range | 000 to 1 | 1 to 3 | 3 to 5 | 5 to 7 |
| Recommended Needle in Metric Size Range | 1.5 to 2.25 mm | 2.25 to 3.25 mm | 3.25 to 3.75 mm | 3.75 to 4.5 mm |

*These are guidelines only. The above reflect the most commonly used gauges and needle sizes for specific yarn categories.*

# Resources

Contact the following companies to find shops that carry the yarns in this book.

**Blue Sky Alpacas, Inc.**
www.blueskyalpacas.com
*Alpaca Silk*

**Cascade Yarns**
www.cascadeyarns.com
*Heritage*

**Coats and Clark**
www.coatsandclark.com
*Heart & Sole*

**Jojoland**
www.jojoland.com
*Melody*

**Lion Brand Yarn**
www.lionbrand.com
*Sock-Ease*

**Mountain Colors**
www.mountaincolors.com
*Bearfoot*

**Royale Hare**
www.royalehare.com
*Hand-Painted High Twist Sock Yarn*

**Skacel Collection, Inc.**
www.skacelknitting.com
Distributor for Austerman Step
*Step das Original*

**Westminster Fibers, Inc.**
www.westminsterfibers.com
Distributor for Regia
*6-ply Country Color and 4-ply*

# Acknowledgments

There are many people that I owe a great deal to, and although I will never be able to thank them enough for their help and contributions, I would like to recognize some very special people.

To everyone at Martingale & Company for the hard work and dedication given to bringing *Terrific Toe-Up Socks* to the bookshelves: my heartfelt thanks to all of you. What a great group of people to work with.

**Karen Soltys,** acquisitions and development editor. Thank you so much for asking me to write a follow-up to *Toe-Up Techniques for Hand-Knit Socks*. I truly did enjoy this project, and if not for you, it never would have happened. Thank you for another great experience.

**Cathy Reitan,** author liaison. Thanks for all your help and for keeping things rolling smoothly.

**Ursula Reikes,** editor. Thank you so much for your patience in working with me and putting up with kinks in the time line. Your expertise in transitioning and clarifying words and instructions is absolutely amazing.

**Timothy Maher,** illustrator. Thank you for creating illustrations that are realistic and true to life so that the knitter is able to visualize and work with my instructions. I truly believe you know more about the lines and flow of knitting stitches than any non-knitter I've ever met.

**Patricia Simkowski, Rozetta (Bee) Hahn, Lois Blanchard, and Kim Ogle,** great friends and wonderful knitters. Thank you for proofing patterns and knitting models for this book. You guys are great!

# About the Author and Illustrator

**Janet Rehfeldt** has been knitting and crocheting since the age of seven. She is the owner of Knitted Threads Designs, LLC. As an instructor, designer, and author, she teaches on both a local and national level, and her designs can be found in leading knitting and crochet publications. She is the author of *More Crocheted Socks* (2010), *Toe-Up Techniques for Hand-Knit Socks* (2008), and *Crocheted Socks: 16 Fun-to-Stitch Patterns* (2003), from Martingale & Company. She lives in Sun Prairie, Wisconsin, with her husband.

**Tim Maher** has a bachelor's degree from the University of Illinois in industrial design and is the principal of Twin Dog Design. His previous illustration and design work includes training materials for the nuclear industry and toy design. After becoming a stay-at-home dad, Tim pursued freelance graphic-design work, which led to illustrations, logo designs, and cover art for various clients and numerous crafts publications. He lives with his family in Florida.

*There's More Online!*

*Find more books about knitting and crocheting at www.martingale-pub.com.*